MW01630127

THIS BOOK IS DEDICATED TO...my sweet boys, adorable nieces/nephews and all of your precious friends...Your love of Christmas and the magic of Santa inspired me to write this book. May you always believe in the true meaning of Christmas. I love you all!

THANK YOU...to all of my family, friends and contributors who helped make this dream a reality! I am forever thankful to each and everyone of you. A special thank you to Linda and Randy King for leading us through this journey.

Ssshh...Santa's Secret Society...
Where Secrets are Unlocked and the Magic of Santa Lives on Forever!
Copyright © 2012 All rights reserved.

No part of this publication may be used, reproduced in whole or in part, stored in a retrieval system, or transmitted in any form or by any means, electronic, mechanical, photocopying, recording, or otherwise, without written permission from the author.

Disclaimer: The purpose of the book is for entertainment purposes only. The author and Magical Transitions shall have neither liability nor responsibility to any person or entity with respect to any loss or damage caused, or alleged to have been caused, directly or indirectly, by the information contained in this book.

A NOTE TO PARENTS...
This book reveals the "real" secret identity of Santa Claus.
Please handle this book with care so it does not end up in a little one's hands.

Illustration Credits:
Hand-Drawn Illustrations by Alexa Stine
Cover: chuntise/istockphoto.com
Several images are courtesy bigstock.com

ISBN # 978-0-615-55814-1

Printed in the United States of America

Written By
Julie Atkinson

Illustrated by
Alexa Stine

About the Author: Julie Atkinson

From the holiday decorations, spending time with her family, and the magical secret's...in Julie's mind, Christmas is simply the most wonderful time of the year. She is married to her wonderful husband, Mike, and together they completely adore their two little elves (I mean boys), Chaz & Cruz. Julie wrote this book for her children and wanted to share it with others as a way to help parents explain the secret of Santa Claus to their own children when the time is right. Julie feels truly blessed to have shared the "secret" with her older son, Chaz, and yet still gets to enjoy the "magic" of Santa with her littlest, Cruz.

About the Illustrator: Alexa Stine

Lexi can be found in Flagstaff, Arizona working independently on art as a resident artist at MELT Flagstaff. This book is her first published piece of art and she thanks all the influences - both positive and negative in her life, they have shaped her into the happy individual she is today.

When the time is right
not a moment too soon…
become part of the magic
it has been waiting for you.

Santa Claus brings lots of presents and joy,

to all of the good girls and boys.

But how can it happen
in one single night…

Can one jolly Santa
make such a flight?

Could it be a very fast sleigh…

or maybe it's the
reindeer you say.

With millions of children counting on him,
Santa will need help…
so let the truth begin.

Santa's Secret Society has been waiting for you,
now that you're older
there's only one thing to do.

But before we can share this magical secret…
you must make a promise
that you will always keep it!

With a pinky swear and a turn of the page,

You are part of a secret
that always must stay.

What if we tell you the magic still exists…

But there are way
more Santas than one,
that fulfills Christmas lists.

Who are these Santas
that make dreams come true?

Well…Santas are moms and dads…grandparents, too!

Even older brothers and sisters join in the fun,

because making Christmas special takes everyone!

Are you ready for the
most exciting
news of the season?

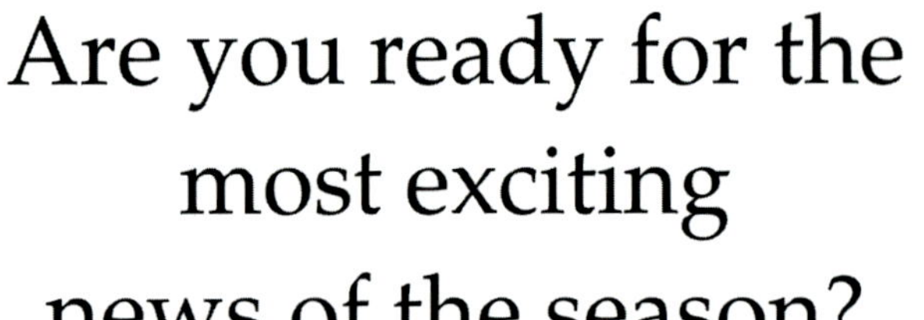

You have been chosen for a very special reason.

You will be able to help make special wishes come true,

because from this point on…

You, are a Santa too!

Lots of little ones are counting on you,
so don't be the one
that makes them go BOO HOO.

If you hear others spreading that he isn't real,
just remember how that would make you feel.
There is a time and a place for the secret
to be shared,
and it's no one's business to say when or where.

So what do you do when
you see Santa at the mall…

Wave with excitement
and smile real big,
for playing along is part
of the "Santa Secret" gig.

Remember to help those in need,
because Christmas is more than "what's in it for me?"

So every year make someone else's wishes come true,
because that is what a good Santa would do.

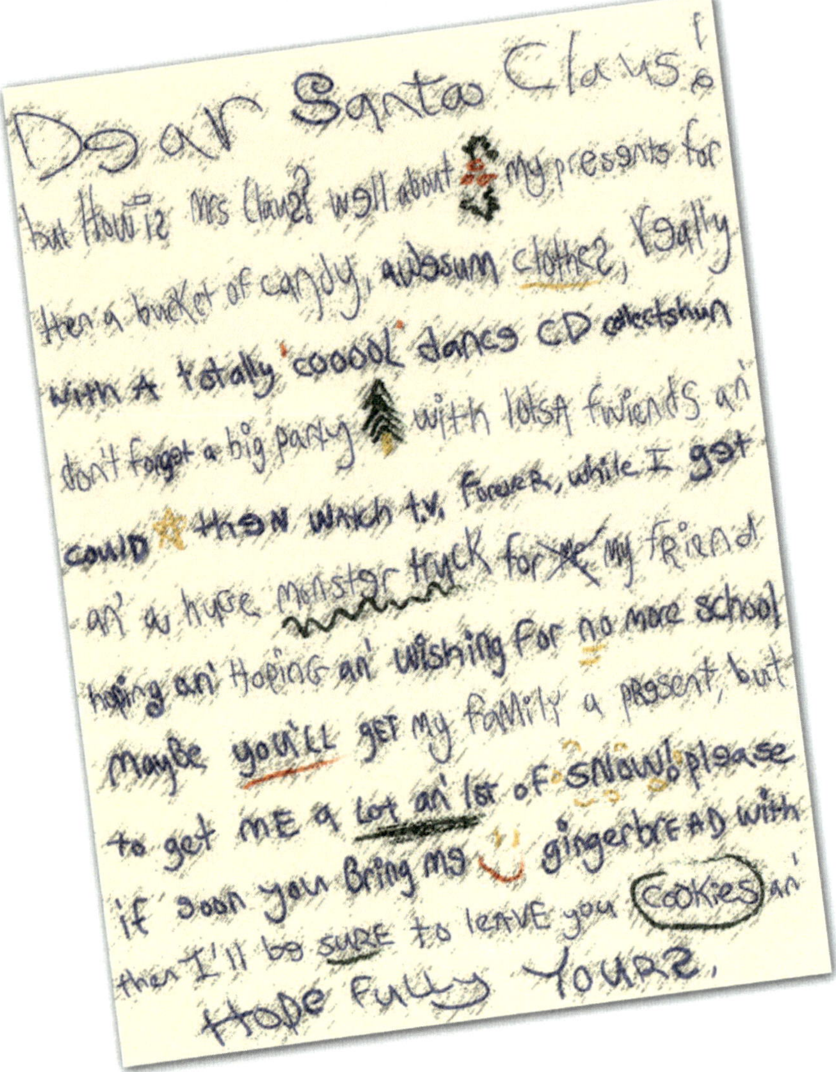

Good thing you made all those Christmas lists,
just think of the love that went into your gifts.

There will be plenty of presents still under the tree,
for the magic of Christmas always will be!

Now how many children are able to say…

that they helped out with Christmas Day?

Santa's Secret Society
has given you the key,
and hopefully your heart
will be filled with glee.

Not everyone gets to be part of the secret,
because some can't be trusted
to keep the "Santa Secret."

Being one of the Santas can be so great,
from dashing around and staying up late.

The cookies and milk will be calling your name,
so eat up…it's part of the game!

Each and every year more children can say…
that they helped make Christmas a magical day!

I made Christmas of __________ magical by__________________________________

____

____

____

____

____

So take this book and lock the magical secret away…

so no one can find it
until their special day.

On Christmas Eve night, when all are asleep,
and not one soul is making a peep…

Believe in the magic you always have known…
for your own special Santa,
still comes when you're grown!

The magical key ornament should
be hung on your tree,
and every year you will be able to see…

The year you became
part of the secret,
and the age you were when
you promised to keep it!

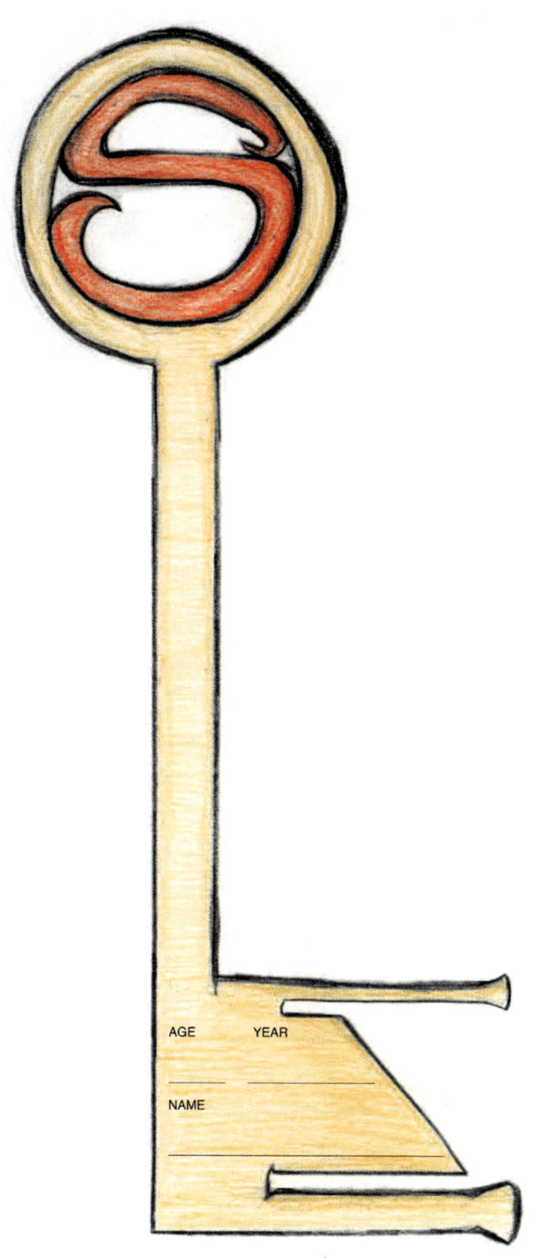

AGE   YEAR
NAME

The magic of Christmas will live on forever…

just sign below

with a promise to never

spread the secret of Santa to someone small

and the joy of Christmas will continue for all!

***Our Family's Promise to have the
Magic of Christmas last FOREVER!***

Official Santa's Secret Society Member…

<table>
<tr><td></td></tr>
</table>

| Name | Date | Age |

Made in the USA
Coppell, TX
03 November 2023

23764095R00029